JEET HEER

IN LOVE WITH ART

FRANÇOISE MOULY'S ADVENTURES IN COMICS WITH ART SPIEGELMAN

COACH HOUSE BOOKS, TORONTO

copyright © Jeet Heer, 2013

first edition

 Canada Council   Conseil des Arts
for the Arts   du Canada

Published with the generous assistance of the Canada Council for the
Arts and the Ontario Arts Council. Coach House Books also acknowledges
the support of the Government of Canada through the Canada Book
Fund and the Government of Ontario through the Ontario Book Publishing Tax Credit.

LIBRARY AND ARCHIVES CANADA CATALOGUING IN PUBLICATION

Heer, Jeet, author
    In love with art : Françoise Mouly's adventures in comics with Art
Spiegelman / written by Jeet Heer.

(Exploded views)
Issued in print and electronic formats.
ISBN 978-1-55245-278-3 (PBK)-- ISBN 978-1-77056-351-3 (EPUB)

    1. Mouly, Françoise--Interviews. 2. Spiegelman, Art--Interviews. 3.
Graphic artists--United States--Interviews. 4. Cartoonists--United States-
-Interviews. 5. Periodical editors--United States--Interviews. I. Title.

NC1429.M69H43 2013   741.5'973   C2013-904099-4

In Love with Art is available as an ebook: ISBN 978 1 77056 351 3.

Purchase of the print version of this book entitles you to a free digital
copy. To claim your ebook of this title, please email sales@chbooks.com
with proof of purchase or visit chbooks.com/digital. (Coach House Books
reserves the right to terminate the free download offer at any time.)

For Robin and Bella, book lovers both

Françoise Mouly.
Portrait of the editor/publisher as a young printer, circa 1977.

The Author's Preface

In 2004, I wrote a newspaper column in the *National Post* arguing that Art Spiegelman, the cartoonist who crafted the graphic memoir *Maus*, is not only a great artist but also a tremendously influential editor. My contention was that *RAW*, the magazine Spiegelman co-edited with his wife, Françoise Mouly, was the seedbed for the efflorescence of the comics form that had started in the 1980s. 'Like all great editors, Spiegelman and Mouly have performed an essential taste-making task, testing out new work with their own refined palates and offering deeply informed guidance to the public,' I wrote. 'Leaving Mouly aside for a second, it is easy to see that Spiegelman's editing is an outgrowth of his intense historical consciousness, his awareness of how comics have evolved and where they need to go.'

My partner, Robin Ganev, rightly challenged both the formulation and thinking behind the last sentence: 'Leaving Mouly aside for a second ...' Why should Mouly be left aside? Hadn't Mouly been as important as Spiegelman as editor of *RAW*? After *RAW*, hadn't Mouly gone on to have an equally impressive career as art editor of the *New Yorker*, where, starting in 1993, she has been responsible for some of the most contentious and admired magazine covers of our time? And hadn't I met innumerable cartoonists who confided to me that Mouly was the best, most thoughtful and incisive editor they've ever worked with? Why was I so quick to relegate Mouly to the status of a clause in a sentence where her husband enjoyed centre stage?

I had no adequate response to these criticisms, and they got me thinking about the sexism of my article and the imbalance of attention given to Mouly and Spiegelman. Spiegelman is famous and Mouly is largely unknown, except to the cartooning cognoscenti. Journalists and academics love writing about Spiegelman. Not only is *Maus* meaty fare for analysis, but Spiegelman himself is an ideal interview subject, gifted with the ability to talk in quips that are both funny and intellectually stimulating.

Beyond the shadow cast by Spiegelman's fame, Mouly's invisibility springs from her gender, her profession and her milieu. As a culture, we still undervalue women, even (or perhaps especially) those as accomplished as Mouly. Editing, her chosen career, involves doing backstage work; it's an invisible profession, often made up of invisible women. And the comics field, which Mouly played a crucial role in remaking, has long been even more hostile to women than the culture at large. Mouly's achievements, remarkable in themselves, are even more impressive given the hurdles she's faced.

My neglect of Mouly is, sadly, nothing new. For every article on Mouly, there are at least a hundred profiles of her husband. *The Comics Journal*, the leading critical magazine in the field, has conducted novel-length interviews with Spiegelman, most of the major *RAW* artists and even a few *RAW* interns who have since gone on to prominence as cartoonists, editors and educators. They've never once published a solo interview with Mouly. (The magazine's editors did have an extended conversation with Spiegelman and Mouly in 1980, but the cartoonist rather than his wife was the clear focus of the discussion).

My 2004 column was not just sexist but also journalistically stupid, because Mouly's career, which I already knew in broad outlines but hadn't fully investigated, raised all sorts of intriguing questions that any wide-awake writer should've keyed into: how did Mouly, born in France in 1955, come to play such an outsized role in North American comics? How did she and Spiegelman successfully transform the public perception of comics, a long-marginalized art form? How was she able to so radically remake the public face of the *New Yorker*, a magazine notoriously resistant to change?

Françoise Mouly has a fascinating story, which I and other writers have neglected to tell. This book – based largely on interviews with Mouly, her husband and key artists she's worked with – is an attempt to redress that omission. Aside from fresh interviews, I've made extensive use of secondary sources. As this book will make clear, the editor I was so thoughtlessly willing to 'leave aside' in my 2004 article has had a career that commands attention.

1

The Invisible Woman

One afternoon in March 1993 in Manhattan, two powerhouses of the magazine world, Tina Brown and Françoise Mouly, met to discuss remaking the *New Yorker*, probably the most venerable periodical in America. They came from strikingly different backgrounds and had, arguably, entirely different ambitions, but they had in common an ability to generate controversy and bring visionary change to their medium. Born and raised in the U.K., the contentious and flamboyant Brown, then thirty-nine, had previously reinvigorated both *Tatler* and *Vanity Fair*, and she had been hired in July 1992 to similarly inject some life into the *New Yorker*, which had become somewhat stagnant and self-satisfied under her predecessors. The then-thirty-seven-year-old Mouly, for her part, was running her own publishing company, RAW Books and Graphics, and for the decade previous to this meeting, had been the co-editor, along with her husband, cartoonist Art Spiegelman, of *RAW*, a magazine that had revolutionized the world of comics by bringing to the form a new level of graphic intensity and artistic seriousness without losing popular appeal. Not least among its achievements, *RAW* serialized Spiegelman's *Maus*, a long-form comic-book story that played a pivotal role in creating the new genre popularly known as 'the graphic novel.'

Brown had already introduced several controversial new features to the *New Yorker*: photography, more celebrity- and news-driven pieces, and topical covers that were a far cry from the tasteful, quiet illustrations the magazine had been favouring. Even more than book jackets, magazine covers serve as both the public face of a publication and its most effective marketing tool; captivating, even scandalous, covers were a clear signal of Brown's intentions. Art Spiegelman created the most provocative of those early covers for the 1993 Valentine's Day issue: an illustration of a Hasidic man kissing a black woman, a sly comment on ethnic tensions that had been erupting in Brooklyn's Crown Heights neighbourhood. The cover, predictably, sparked outrage, but it also made people talk about the *New Yorker* in a way they hadn't

Art Spiegelman's *New Yorker* cover for February 15, 1993,
titled *Valentine's Day*. One of the earliest New Yorker covers
to tackle explosive political and social issues.

been doing for years. For Brown, the key to successful publishing was generating buzz: she wanted the *New Yorker* to be the talk of the town, and the Spiegelman cover certainly achieved that goal.

Brown asked Spiegelman to recommend art directors who could help her come up with covers that would keep up the buzz. He provided a list. Brown was also bouncing around ideas with Lawrence Weschler, who had profiled Spiegelman for *Rolling Stone* in 1986 and served as Brown's informal advisor. She asked Weschler why he thought Spiegelman hadn't included his own wife; Mouly and Brown had met once before at the office of RAW Books and Graphics, when Spiegelman was working on the interracial kiss cover, and Brown had been very impressed by the issues of *RAW* she saw there. It hadn't occurred to either Spiegelman or Mouly that they'd be interested in someone with Mouly's unconventional background. Weschler told Mouly Brown was considering hiring her.

A staff position at the *New Yorker* is a dream for many writers, artists and editors, but Mouly didn't initially leap at the opportunity; she had mixed feelings about both Brown and the magazine. As Mouly says, 'I heard Tina was brought in to the *New Yorker* at a dinner party in the summer of 1992, and I couldn't understand why everyone was so excited and opinionated about it. The *New Yorker* meant nothing to me except for being the place I sent artists I thought were too staid for *RAW*.'

Nor was Mouly impressed by the fact that Brown, as editor of *Vanity Fair*, had published a photo on the June 1985 cover showing an elegant Ronald and Nancy Reagan dancing during the presidential inaugural ball, accompanied by a gushing essay celebrating the couple penned by William F. Buckley, Jr. In *RAW*, Mouly and Spiegelman had frequently published comics that abrasively challenged the right-wing turn of American culture under Reagan. 'I hated Brown's *Vanity Fair* cover that had the Reagans dancing,' Mouly recalls. 'That was the enemy speaking, glamorizing a rearguard reactionary who was starting a grand squeeze of the middle class for the benefit of the super rich.'

But despite her political reservations, Mouly liked Brown personally. 'I was impressed by her when she came down to the office,' Mouly remembers. 'She's very charismatic, quick-witted, full of energy.' And like Brown herself, Mouly was thrilled by the firestorm of controversy Spiegelman's cover ignited. Both women had a strong visual sense and appreciated the power of images to stir debate. Nor was a love of inflammatory imagery the only thing the women had in common: both were dynamos, famous for pushing both themselves and the artists they worked with. Spiegelman describes Mouly as a 'whirling dervish,' someone always feverishly working on many projects at once. It was a good match.

Yet a *New Yorker* job would mean becoming an employee. Accustomed to being her own boss, and more at home with subversive art than subservient work, Mouly didn't want to be just an employee at a mass-market magazine trying to please subscribers: 'It really was visceral,' she explains. 'Why would I want to be somebody's secretary?' As she thought it over and discussed the possible job with friends, her feelings changed. Brown wasn't seeking just assistance, she realized, but rather Mouly's singular expertise. 'If Tina Brown knew what she wanted, she wouldn't be asking me,' Mouly said.

Mouly set about studying the magazine's visual history (aided by the fact that Weschler gave her access to the magazine's library). No admirer of its recent covers, which tended to the pastoral and decorative, she was delighted to discover that during its first few decades the front of the magazine had been dominated by flashy, poster-like images of New York life obviously inspired by one of the great French cartoon magazines of the early twentieth century, *L'Assiette au Beurre*. (Harold Ross, the *New Yorker*'s founder, had been a soldier in France in World War I, where he likely encountered the country's rich graphic culture, just as he had been influenced by American humour magazines such as *Judge* and *Life*.) To reshape the front of the *New Yorker* as a contemporary, American version of *L'Assiette au Beurre*, with each cover an exuberant cartoon commentary on the world? That was an ambition that Mouly could put her heart into. 'Harold Ross and Tina Brown were both visual editors,' Mouly concluded.

Spontaneously, she drew up a proposal that argued the *New Yorker* should return to having artists as featured contributors, with not just more daring covers but also an increased use of photos and illustrations inside the magazine to be integrated with the prose and poetry. Soon after sending in the proposal, Mouly got a call to meet Brown for lunch.

That auspicious meal took place at the Royalton, a boutique hotel and Brown haunt close to the headquarters of Condé Nast, which owned the *New Yorker*. 'I knew what I wanted to do and was in a take-it-or-leave-it mode,' Mouly says. 'If it didn't work for Tina, that was fine with me. If she took it, I knew it would be a challenge, but it was an exciting one.' Mouly's main concern was how she would reconcile a high-powered job with raising her two kids, a daughter almost five and a son who had just turned one. Mouly thought about asking if the job could be delayed for a year, but knew the request would be rejected.

Mouly's proposal was barely discussed during the lunch; Brown had clearly made up her mind. Like Mouly, she was a mother of two and, at one point in their conversation, she looked at Mouly and asked, 'Do you have a good babysitter?' Mouly took the job.

The move from *RAW* to the *New Yorker* followed a pattern that had governed her life and career: a semi-steady course from the margins of culture to its centres of power. When Mouly first started publishing comics, they were a fringe and sometimes derided medium. Her tenure at *RAW* changed that, bringing attention and credibility to the form. Working at the *New Yorker* allowed her to further pursue her aesthetic agenda on one of the most prestigious stages in the world.

Even before taking on that challenge, Mouly was, by any estimation, an exceedingly illustrious and talented editor. She's had as massive and transformative an impact on comics as Ezra Pound had on modernist literature, Max Perkins on early-twentieth-century American novels or Gordon Lish on contemporary fiction. At *RAW*, she brought to comics the stringent and demanding conceptualism of modern art while remaining true to the form's democratic appeal as a mass art. She infused a staid *New Yorker* with an eye-catching, often eye-popping, cartoon aesthetic and added a whole new stratum of narrative meaning. More recently, and concurrent with her *New Yorker* work, Mouly founded TOON Books, a publishing outfit that is likewise revitalizing the formerly moribund field of children's comics.

If Mouly is so impressive a figure in the world of of comics and magazine editing, why have her achievements so rarely received the attention they deserve? Sexism is undeniably a factor. All too many journalistic and critical accounts speak of 'Art Spiegelman's *RAW* magazine' as if he did the editorial heavy lifting all by himself. This sexism exists in the culture at large but is particularly intense in the comics world, a subculture notorious, at least until recent years, for its nerdy 'no girls allowed' attitude. As Mouly notes, during her first few decades in comics she would routinely go to conventions that were more than 90 percent male and where she was often brushed off as an unwelcome interloper.

Another factor is simply the nature of her work. Mouly is an editor. A cartoonist or writer makes visible marks for all to see. Part of an editor's job is to disappear, to let the artist speak for himself or herself; editing has, in fact, been called 'the invisible art.' This book will try to make the invisible visible to show how Mouly's editorial fingerprints can be seen on every project she works on. She brings rigour and imagination to the craft of editing, and in doing so proves that editing can be more than a craft – it is, at its best, an art.

2

A Surgeon's Daughter

Françoise Mouly was born to disappoint her parents. She was particularly a bitter pill for her formidable father, Dr. Roger Mouly. A pioneer in popularizing plastic surgery in France, Dr. Mouly had made a name for himself not just as a much sought-after practitioner but also as a theorist and advocate of surgically modifying and improving the human body. With a colleague, he developed the Dufourmentel-Mouly method of breast reduction, which uses a lateral incision that leaves a smaller scar than earlier procedures. An expert whose wisdom was sought by both highly specialized medical journals and newspapers like *Le Monde*, a charismatic and flashy Parisian who managed to charm both conservative politicians such as Jacques Chirac and the student radicals who took to the streets in 1968, a venerated professional who served as the vice-president of the Société internationale de chirurgie esthétique and was inducted as a Chevalier de la Légion d'honneur, Dr. Mouly thought he lacked only one thing to make his life complete and meaningful: a son who could inherit his practice and continue to make the Mouly name synonymous with French plastic surgery.

Françoise Mouly, the second of three daughters, made her unwelcome entrance into the world in 1955. 'Both my parents had a very explicit complaint which they kept bringing up over and over again: that the worst thing that ever happened to them was to have three daughters,' Mouly recalls somewhat sarcastically. 'They only wanted to have a son. They put up with my older sister, but by the time I was born my father was so disappointed he nearly did not declare me at the town hall. A few years later my little sister was born, and shame again. My parents were crushed.' (Mouly is one year younger than her sister Laurence and six years older than Marie-Pierre, whose name is a memorial to the desire for a son who would have been named Pierre).

That heavy burden of parental discontent aside, Mouly's parents provided her with particular kinds of inspiration. Prior to her marriage to Dr. Mouly, Josée Giron had been a stewardess at

TWA. It was a chic and sexy profession at the time (but one reserved for single women), and Mouly says now that her appreciation of beauty is very much tied to her sense of her mother as a 'truly beautiful, graceful, elegant and glamorous person.' Even as a child, Mouly wanted to create art beautiful enough to suit Giron: 'A lot of my early memories as a kid have to do with making objects and paintings for her.'

If her mother's elegance and grace kindled Mouly's aesthetic awareness, her early education gave shape to these interests through a holistic curriculum that combined writing, drawing and reciting. At the beginning of each class, as their homeroom teacher recited a poem, students using crow quill pens copied it out in calligraphic writing on the right side of their notebooks. On the left side, they illustrated the poem. Finally, at the bottom of the page, they were instructed to draw a geometric frieze. The lesson concluded with the students memorizing the poem – not just by rote, but with the passion and emotion of elocutionists.

'It was really great,' she says now. 'It combined the beauty of the words and the calligraphy with images, including the frieze, which had to be in keeping with the mood of the poetry. It brought together literature, memorization and acting out. That's all good training for a very full experience of the power of art and literature.' While this artistic education had broader purposes, it's hard to think of better training for a future editor of comics and illustration.

Aside from newspapers and magazines, neither Roger Mouly nor Josée Giron read much. The only books young Françoise ever received from her family were hand-me-down Jules Verne and Alexandre Dumas volumes from her mother's childhood library. But as a child Mouly loved to read – it was 'the one activity that protected me from my family and from anything in school,' she says – and she craved books, particularly the lavishly illustrated fairy-tale treasuries offered as prizes for top students. 'French schooling is very consistent in never giving you anything but negative reinforcement,' Mouly explains. 'You get threatened all the time. Everyone is always ceaselessly ranked. You have exams every single day.' Ferociously competitive, Mouly's goal every year was to earn the large hardcover that was first prize. 'It was something I treasured,' she says. 'I read the stories and reread the stories and looked at the illustrations for hours.'

Illustrated fairy tales were a precursor to the comics she discovered a few years later. As a preteen, she loved to accompany her father to the newsstand, where he would buy Mouly the latest issue of *Pilote*, a weekly anthology best known for featuring the squat, quick-witted Gaul Astérix, whose rollicking adventures in the ancient world were then at the height of their popularity. René Goscinny, co-creator of *Astérix* and editor-in-chief of *Pilote*, was much influenced by Harvey Kurtzman – the mastermind behind the early *Mad* comics and *Mad* magazine – and Mouly loved the satirical, *Mad*-inspired sections of *Pilote*, which also included the Kurtzman-inflected work of Marcel Gotlib, whose strip *La Rubrique-à-Brac* she especially cherished. (She read dutifully, but with little pleasure, the melodramatic adventure series found on adjoining pages, notably Jean Giraud's solidly drawn but clichéd Wild West strip *Blueberry*.)

Magazines such as *Pilote* were the mainstay of French cartooning, but they were increasingly supplemented with wildly popular hardcover albums – both Hergé's beloved boy hero *Tintin* and *Astérix* were available in this format. The typical album was sixty-four pages, thin but sturdily bound, and printed on white matte paper. The format was an offshoot of French children's books, and the volumes were designed, like quality kids' books, to withstand multiple readings. Mouly didn't own very many of these albums, but she read them all the time at the houses of friends. And while they were relatively formulaic and predictable – especially compared to the always surprising books Mouly would create later in life – they were an early attempt to intelligently marry elegant book design with comics. And they stood in stark contrast to the disposable comic books then printed on cheap newsprint in North America. As Art Spiegelman notes, his French cartooning counterparts started off with a natural advantage: 'They didn't have crappy ten-cent comics, they had *Tintin* albums to lean on.'

Though she was not the son they wanted, Dr. Mouly was well aware that his middle daughter was a stellar student, and

Françoise was soon being groomed to take over the plastic surgery practice. She was pushed toward medical studies; novels and poetry were replaced, to her dismay, by math and physics. As a teenager, she spent some of her vacations training in her father's office. Initially she helped her father write research papers on melonoma, and by the time she was twenty she was in the operating room, where she would concentrate on her father's hands – a valuable lesson in creativity. 'The precision of his sutures and scars was really magical,' Mouly says now. 'Surgical gestures have to have elegance and an economy of means. You don't just cut and see what happens. You have to really think about it before you make that one blade penetrate the flesh.'

The pleasure of working with her hands, of reshaping the world through touch, never left Mouly. And it's certainly no accident that some of the artists she later collaborated with, notably Charles Burns, work with images obsessed with anatomy and relentlessly portray the human body as a radically mutable thing. Burns's horror/romance mashup 'A Marriage Made in Hell' (first published in *RAW* no. 6 in 1984) features a woman whose badly charred body is mistakenly transformed into the opposite gender, a case of reconstructive surgery gone unbearably wrong. Of course this subject matter resonated with Mouly; it's not much of a metaphoric stretch to say that, as an editor and book designer, she ultimately did become a kind of surgeon, nipping and folding pieces of paper rather than human skin. The tools she learned to use in the surgical theatre are the same she uses at her drafting table: markers, knives, scissors. As Spiegelman notes, about the editing of *RAW*, 'Françoise was uncannily skilful with X-Acto blades and making hand separations with Zip-A-Tone, cutting Zip-A-Tone strips an eighth of an inch wide, often angled on three overlays to avoid moiré patterns.' And, eventually, she would give that most esteemed of grand dames, the *New Yorker*, a face lift.

Mouly might have stuck with her medical education, she says, if she'd felt her father was a 'real doctor' who helped people. Dr. Mouly did occasionally reconstruct the bodies of those who had been scarred or burned, but his daughter was troubled by much

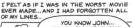

A page from Charles Burns's 'A Marriage Made In Hell' from *RAW* no. 6 (1984). A story about reconstructive surgery gone awry, edited by a woman who was once encouraged to become a plastic surgeon.

of what the profession entailed. 'I had a moral problem with plastic surgery,' she says. 'I saw it as frivolous and downright damaging to people. No amount of surgical procedure can give you a sense of being at peace with your body. Plastic surgery exploits insecurity to such a high degree.' Mouly's objections dovetailed with her own growing political consciousness. She turned thirteen in 1968, a fateful year in France, when extraordinary student and labour protests engulfed the country. At the height of the demonstrations, during three weeks in May, President Charles de Gaulle's government brought in tanks, placing Paris in a near state of siege designed to intimidate the protestors. Many Parisians, including Mouly's mother and sisters, fled the city. Dr. Mouly, however, insisted on staying to look after his patients – as a doctor, he had access to gas coupons when fuel was being rationed – and he kept his daughter/assistant with him.

Prior to 1968, Mouly's Paris had consisted mainly of her neighbourhood in the 17th arrondissement, a sleepy haven for professionals Mouly compares to New York's Upper East Side. The Moulys lived in an apartment on the fourth floor, with the third reserved for Dr. Mouly's practice. (His three daughters were constantly being told to keep quiet when patients were being seen.) The protests, however, revealed an entirely new, and thrilling, city – for the first time, she visited the Latin Quarter, the heart of the unrest, and other bohemian haunts. The 'communal spirit' of 1968 was infectious. 'I was philosophically taken by the anarchists,' she says. 'I painted quite a few A's in circles.' As with many members of the *soixante-huitard* generation, Mouly was an avid reader of the anarcho-left-wing weekly *Hara-Kiri Hebdo*, although she found its politics better expressed in its cartoons than its articles.

In 1970, Mouly was sent to a boarding school, the Lycée Jeanne d'Arc, in central France, and brought the spirit of May '68, still strong in many parts of the country, with her. She encouraged her fellow high school students to join demonstrations with local university students, where they enthusiastically chanted the slogan 'L'union fait la force' ('Unity makes strength'). 'I was expelled something like twenty-four or twenty-five times because I was trying to drag everybody into demonstrations,' she says. Jeanne d'Arc was an appropriate school for Mouly; as Spiegelman would later say, she has a Joan of Arc side – a passionate desire to save the world.

Mouly returned to Paris to earn her baccalaureate, and the next year she disappointed her father again by enrolling in the architecture program at the École nationale supérieure des beaux-arts. Even though it was a profession that made use of her mathematical and scientific training, and in which she would work with her hands, it thwarted Dr. Mouly's plan. Though he lived till 2008, 'In his entire life, my father never forgave me,' Mouly says. 'He was so, so disappointed. He never abandoned the dream that I would be a surgeon. I had already published a few issues of *RAW* and he still said it was not too late.'

She adored being at the Beaux-Arts, and moved to the Latin Quarter with her then-boyfriend, Jean-Robert, a wildly creative though impractical young man who had started his architecture studies the year before. (Spiegelman for his part claims that all of Mouly's ex-boyfriends were named Jean-something.)

The program at her architecture 'atelier' was appealingly hands-on. 'I loved the basic training where they give you an assignment like, "Build a school,"' she says. 'You can't just start sketching. It's a very systematic process where you have to first come up with a concept. You have to take in all of the information about the constraints; you have to analyze the geology, the geography, the economy and as much of the context as you can. In architecture you can't just say, "Oh, I'll put this window next to that door." You have to find a dominant idea or concept and then everything – from the light socket to the facade – becomes an expression of that concept.'

Mouly was enchanted by the loopy futuristic architect Hans-Walter Müller, who created inflatable structures known as *gonflables* – part art objects, part inhabitable structures – but as she became more familiar with architecture as a career, she learned such fanciful design was not common. There was a serious discrepancy between the idealistic notions she was taught at school, where students were encouraged to see themselves as artists, and the commercial straitjacket that tightly bound the actual profession. 'It was far more interesting as a set of studies than as a practice, because in practice you are a cog in the machinery,' Mouly observes. 'There are only a few name architects and those people spend all their time selling themselves.' To be a successful architect you have to run an office with a team and take many assignments to keep the firm going. It wasn't a life Mouly could imagine for herself.

In 1974, Mouly's disenchantment with architecture was aggravated by a series of personal crises. She had broken up with Jean-Robert but kept running into him because they were at adjacent schools. And the family was disintegrating as her parents went through what she calls 'the bloodiest divorce on earth.' While Giron would eventually reinvent herself, with great success, as an art book dealer, real estate agent, ghost writer (with at least one bestseller to her credit) and interior designer – an unusual career arc that would also inspire Mouly – mother and daughter had an occasionally nettlesome relationship. (Spiegelman says when he first met his mother-in-law, she took him aside to make fun of Mouly for lacking sufficient cooking and domestic skills.) Mouly needed to get away from France.

Travel was one way out. As a teenager she had been, in Spiegelman's words, 'a weirdly adventurous traveller.' In 1972, she, Jean-Robert and two other architecture students hopped in a van for a two-and-a-half-month adventure that included an excursion to Afghanistan. Two years later she made a solo trip to Algeria to study vernacular architecture, which she's always been interested in. 'I was supposed to go with my sister, Laurence, but she dumped me and stayed with a friend in Marseilles,' Mouly explains. 'So I had to board the boat and take the trip alone. I ended up in the M'zab, in the middle of the Sahara, where Le Corbusier had been. It was the trip from hell, travelling alone in a Muslim country. I got robbed of money and passport. The police laughed at me because only a whore would be travelling alone, so that would teach me, but, anyway, I did a great study, one of the most exciting things I did in school.'

Aside from these venturesome journeys, she also made the hostel rounds all over Europe, travelling to Italy, Spain, Holland, Belgium, England, Germany, Romania, Bulgaria, Turkey and Greece. This time around, she needed to go somewhere she hadn't been before. She decided to take a sabbatical from her architecture studies, got a job as a cleaner at a hotel and saved up enough money for a plane ticket to New York. Unlike many Europeans of her generation, she didn't have a romantic fixation with New York or even American culture. But it was very far away and, to her, alluringly unknown.

Houston Street

Page from Mark Beyer's *Manhattan* (a 'mailbook' designed and published by Mouly in 1978). The grittiness of New York street life in the 1970s and 1980s would be a major topic for many of the comics Mouly published in those decades. Beyer's emphatically primitive art combined a child's view of reality with close attentiveness to urban scruffiness.

3
A Second Birth

Françoise Mouly bustles through life feet first. Her modus operandi is to make life-changing decisions quickly and intuitively, working out the details of execution only after she's committed. Flying alone to New York was a grand and typically Moulian gesture: hurtling herself with minimal preparation into one of the world's great metropolises, being momentarily bewildered and overwhelmed before she finding her footing and finally creating a niche for herself.

She arrived in Manhattan on September 2, 1974, with $200 in her pocket, expecting to stay in a safe, comfortable youth hostel, the sort familiar to European travellers. But through some transatlantic communication mishap, she discovered that the hostel was in fact the mostly male midtown YMCA. A hostile receptionist told the puzzled French visitor to seek shelter elsewhere. Knowing that a taxi and hotel room would quickly exhaust her resources, Mouly held her ground. The Y catered mainly to homeless men, and the single floor reserved for women was full. Grim armed guards (Mouly remembers them as 'goons') were called in and, while the other guests were ordered to stay in their rooms and the corridor cleared, the guards escorted Mouly to a room, where she was locked in. 'I was terrified the first day or two,' Mouly recalls. But the trauma of her arrival was also a rite of passage that she describes now as 'salutary.' 'It was kind of like a second birth for me,' she says. 'In this new world, I was only answerable to myself.'

She was moved to the women's floor on the second day of her stay, but she quickly found a spot at a Salvation Army instead. While her new lodgings were more hospitable, New York itself continued to be both frightening and exhilarating. 'I walked the streets and realized I could get murdered and nobody would ever know,' she says. 'Before I left, my mother said to be really careful when I took a cab because in New York, because when a cab stops at a red light, bandits open the door and cut off your hands with a machete to steal your rings.' Mouly laughs about it now –

both at the fear-mongering image and at the notion that she could afford a cab anyway.

The city was then deep into its mid-seventies nervous breakdown. The grimy dimensions of that civic crisis are well known: the spike in crime, the garbage strewn everywhere, the graffiti-covered subways and burnt-out buildings, the aftermath of a heroin epidemic, slum landlords using arson as a form of ad hoc urban development – all topped off by a financial catastrophe engineered by President Gerald Ford's Treasury Secretary who deliberately squeezed New York into bankruptcy to make a point about fiscal prudence. It's the city notoriously immortalized in Martin Scorsese's *Taxi Driver* as 'an open sewer.'

In spite of this – or perhaps because of it – the New York of that era was very receptive to outsiders – especially when compared to Mouly's native city. 'You think of Paris as an interesting city until you come to New York,' Mouly explains. 'In Paris, everyone is always putting you down for what you don't know.' Mouly found that Manhattan's art circles were accessible to her; she didn't have to flash credentials or call up connections to take part in cultural events. She met a friend of Hans-Walter Müller's, architect and New York University urban studies professor Bernhard Leitner, who introduced her to the experimental films of Stan Brakhage and the Anthology Film Archives, a theatre that specialized in such work. Soon, she was even performing in avant-garde theatre pioneer Richard Foreman's play *Pandering to the Masses* as part of a cast of non-professional actors. Paris was starting to feel not just distant but also parochial.

Within four months of the YMCA fiasco, Mouly found an enviable place to rent, a spacious loft in SoHo, which remains her home base to this day. In 1975, SoHo wasn't the tony address it would become but a slowly gentrifying neighbourhood of light manufacturing firms – a cardboard box factory next to a plastic doll maker, a sweatshop next to a lumberyard – and upper 'loft' floors filled with would-be artists living hand to mouth. Lacking glitter and glamour, SoHo was also much safer than the nightmarish New York Mouly had been warned about in Paris. 'There was no crime in SoHo because there was nothing to steal,' she

and magazine stands. These outlets would sell not just Mouly's map but, on occasion, and on consignment, the postcards, mailbooks and other printed items she was making. Learning about the retail end of the business was invaluable, and she found herself in a new role as a salesperson. She'd finally broken free of her immigrant insecurity and become confident in dealing with people.

Mouly's annual stint on *The Streets of Soho* was akin to Spiegelman's relationship with Topps, and in both cases, the day job seeped into their artistic projects. Mouly and Spiegelman would one day include faux bubble-gum cards as an insert in *RAW* and use maps to distill information in a way that paralleled comics. It is surely no accident that the back cover of *Maus* features two maps that help articulate the book's theme of the impact of the Holocaust on an American childhood: a large map of wartime Europe containing an inset of Rego Park, Queens, where Spiegelman grew up. (Stylistically, this back cover also deliberately echoed the the 1940s and '50s Dell map-back mystery paperbacks). Some of Mouly's favourite *New Yorker* covers are parody maps: notably Maira Kalman and Rick Meyerowitz's depiction of New Yorkistan (December 10, 2001), which re-imagines the five boroughs as Afghan provinces.

With her printing press and newfound confidence as a publisher, as well as a slate of European artists who deserved a wider audience, Mouly was slowly inching toward starting a magazine. But she had one major hurdle to overcome: her reluctant husband. 'Françoise said, "Let's do a magazine,"' Spiegelman recalls, 'and I said, "Feet, do your stuff, get away from here."' The stark limitations of North American comics, however, did make the idea of a new magazine seem not only plausible but urgent. During the late 1970s, Spiegelman had had the frustrating experience of working as an editorial consultant for *High Times* and *Playboy*, finding that both would accept only comics that fit their narrow editorial parameters (drugs and sex, respectively). He was also worried about the fate of artists such as Mark Beyer, who were finding it hard to publish. Some of Beyer's earliest work appeared in *Arcade* but his bleak stories of Amy and Jordan – two doll-like creatures who live in an urban hell of cockroaches

Françoise Mouly, Joost Swarte and Art Spiegelman,
celebrating the publication of postcards, circa 1978.

and psychological turmoil – had been rejected by the few remaining underground publishers. Spiegelman was also now teaching at the School of Visual Arts and wanted a forum for his best students. Most of the vocationally minded students who took Spiegelman's classes had no greater ambition than to draw for Marvel, but he did have a few talented pupils such as Mark Newgarden, Jayr Pulga, Kazimieras G. Prapuolenis (who publishes under the pen name Kaz) and Drew Friedman, who were already doing quirky and personal work that would be sharpened through his editorial guidance.

On the last day of 1979, at a New Year's Eve party ringing in the new decade, Spiegelman decided that the time for caution was over. The couple agreed to launch the magazine they had already spent so much time talking about. But even in agreement there was a mutual misunderstanding that made the decision possible: Spiegelman thought that *RAW* was going to be a one-shot publication – they would do it to show it could be done and then move on – but Mouly, on the other hand, wanted a publication with a future.

6

Postponed Suicides

From its first issue in July 1980, *RAW*'s sheer sumptuousness was dazzling, a feast for the eyes. 'My initial impression was that it was the kind of magazine I had always envisioned a great comics magazine being,' says Charles Burns, who found the first issue in the summer of 1980 in a Manhattan store where it had probably been hand-delivered by Mouly. 'The first thing was the size of it. I responded to that immediately.' The first eight issues were oversize, measuring 10 ½ by 14 ⅛ inches, designed to sit on newsstands alongside such publications as *Interview*, *Wet* and *Slash* – all considered, in eighties parlance, 'New Wave' magazines. These large-size issues tended to feature around twenty contributors per issue, most doing strips of a few pages long. From the second issue onwards, *Maus* was serialized in every issue.

If *RAW* was a more luxurious product than comics readers were used it, it also came at a higher price. 'The first issue was $3.50 and I was like, I don't know if I can afford that, that's expensive,' Burns recalls. At the time a typical superhero newsstand comic cost fifty cents, with the few remaining underground titles selling for $1.25.

July 1980, when *RAW* made its entrance into the world, was the nadir of an unusually bleak period in the history of American comics. The commercial comic-book world was dominated by DC and Marvel, who published largely inane superhero comics and had, through their predatory business practices, driven out of the industry the few real talents they had, notably Jack Kirby, a powerhouse who had dominated the field for decades but who finally concluded that he was happier doing grunt work for Saturday morning cartoon shows. The undergrounds continued their long descent into irrelevance. A few independent comic-book publishers had sprung up, but they tended to rehash trite ideas from other sources: Dave Sim's *Cerebus the Aardvark* was a mashup of *Howard the Duck* and *Conan the Barbarian*, while Wendy Pini's *Elfquest* was simply illustrated Tolkien, but without any of the world-building fertility of the original. Even Kim

Thompson and Gary Groth, who aspired to produce more sophisticated fare with their newly formed Fantagraphics books, had inchoate taste and a tendency toward genre pastiche. One of their earliest publications was *The Flames of Gyro*, a stiff and barely competent imitation of Alex Raymond's 1930s *Flash Gordon* comic strip.

Newspaper comics were similarly barren. A field that had once housed the imaginative wonders of *Little Nemo* and *Krazy Kat* had shrivelled into a gag-a-day format that best suited banal suburban sitcom strips like *Blondie* and *Hi and Lois*. Even Charles Schulz, who had done remarkably personal strips in that format, had entered the long creative decline of his late career. One of the few bright spots on the newspaper page was Gary Larson's freshly launched *The Far Side*, a small flower in the wasteland. Fans of political satire could also enjoy Garry Trudeau's *Doonesbury* and Jules Feiffer's eponymous strip *Feiffer*.

If you cared at all for comics, you could go months without reading anything inspiring or innovative aside from *The Far Side*. Against this grim background, *RAW* was a beacon not just for its intrinsic merits but for illuminating new paths out of the wilderness. In an enthusiastic review in the *Comics Journal*, novelist Carter Scholz urged readers to pick up *RAW* because 'it may be the last thing standing between us and an eternity of *The Incredible Hulk*.'

RAW was so physically lovely that it's tempting to talk about it in purely visual terms. But comics are a narrative medium, and the potency of *RAW* came from the emotional candour (or rawness, if you will) of the stories, not just the production values. In *Breakdowns*, Spiegelman had demonstrated that experimenting with the language of comics wasn't just a cerebral exercise but could help expand the emotional range of the medium. The best comics in *RAW*, including a story by Mouly herself, 'Industry News and Review No. 6', were outgrowths of *Breakdowns* but pushed Spiegelman's ideas to a higher level of intensity and audacity.

As its title suggests, 'Industry News and Review No. 6' takes inspiration from the stencilled, shadowless clip art found in technical newsletters. The first large panel shows a printing plant,

Françoise Mouly's 'Industry News and Review No. 6' from *RAW* no. 1 (1980).
An autobiographical reflection on suicide, printing, the artistic vocation and love.
Mouly's only comic for *RAW*.

with workers involved in various stages of press work. The cropped headline alludes to a 'Heidelberg Speedmaster,' the type of printing press Mouly lusted after but didn't buy. Following this panel, we see a young woman working on this machine, tormented by uncertainty about what to do with her life. 'I hate myself ... I wish I was dead ... ' she thinks. 'And ... it's boring to always feel that way.' The woman starts to engage in a conversation with an off-panel interlocutor who asks, 'Honey could you help me with this?' She thinks, 'Ah, a way out?' After providing the assistance (like much of the action in the comic, this is elliptically alluded to but not presented), she thinks, 'I like being useful.' Still, the woman remains divided about what she's doing, worried that she's 'just a slave.' Asked if she wants to 'work on something of [her] own,' she frets, 'I'm just not an "artist"!' While the woman remains tormented, her worry is answered: the panels themselves are small fragments of the large opening image, and it seems she's working on the very comic strip we are reading.

One way to read 'Industry News and Review No. 6' is as an autobiographical distillation of the uncertainty that Mouly experienced in the late seventies, when she wasn't sure what her vocation was. The resolution of the strip is embodied not just in the image of the Heidelberg – showing that the answer to her dilemma is a publishing career – but also in the magazine that the strip appears, the ultimate solution to the anxieties she voices in her story.

The allusion to suicide at the very beginning of 'Industry News and Review No. 6' is hardly an accident. Suicide was a major unifying theme in the first issue of *RAW*, which was even subtitled 'The Graphix Magazine of Postponed Suicides.' This dark joke was a play on E. M. Cioran's adage that 'every book is a suicide postponed.'

The Cioran quote, Mouly explains, 'was very meaningful for me. It expressed exactly where I was at. I was emerging from a long period of suicidal depression (in my first few years toggling between New York and Paris) into a whole world I passionately wanted to build. And what I wanted to do was a book (or a magazine ...).'

By appropriating Cioran's aphorism, Mouly and Spiegelman explicitly made their personal obsession with self-annihilation part of the governing gestalt of their journal. It shouldn't just be taken as a jape, however – *RAW* was quite literally a way for the couple to stave off death and do something meaningful with their lives.

'Suicide is definitely an interest Françoise and I had in common,' Spiegelman says. 'We both had suicidal streaks.' Mouly had been seduced by Spiegelman's comic about his mother's suicide, and that comic provided the thematic centre to both *Breakdowns* and the graphic novel *Maus*, where it was reprinted as a visually disruptive, but essential, comic within a comic. While *Maus* famously tackles the Holocaust, the trauma and lingering impact of the genocide is made specific and personal by Anja Spiegelman's suicide. The book is structured like a detective story, with Spiegelman trying to solve not just the greatest crime of the twentieth century, but also the riddle of his mother's death. The key moment of emotional tension in the story is when Spiegelman, as detective, angrily discovers that his chief witness, who happens to be his father, has destroyed a crucial bit of evidence, Anja's diary. There are countless Holocaust narratives, but what sets *Maus* apart is its structural ingenuity, its refusal of resolution (Anja's story will never be told) and the fraught family relationships that Spiegelman mercilessly depicts.

Most of the other stories in the first issue of *RAW* touch on suicide either as an plot point or as entertainment, even through jokes. The central story is Jacques Tardi's 'Manhattan,' which features a Parisian who comes to New York, wallows in the squalor of the city like a character out of Louis-Ferdinand Céline or Martin Scorsese, and finally kills himself. Although much more grim than Mouly's own experiences, Tardi's story does capture how disorienting New York can be to outside eyes, a recurring theme in the comics and graphics Mouly has worked on. The first *RAW* also reprinted a Winsor McCay strip from 1906 featuring a man dreaming about jumping off the Brooklyn Bridge – he bounces back and is bopped on the head by a cop.

In a 1980 interview with the *Comics Journal*, Spiegelman argued that suicidal thoughts could be consoling. 'To think about suicide

isn't necessarily to commit suicide,' he contends. 'It's to acknowl-
edge the precariousness of being alive and to affirm it. Every
moment that you don't commit suicide is an affirmation.' To think
about death while finding a way not to die: that paradoxical
stance is one of the most important threads binding together the
Mouly-Spiegelman sensibility.

The quality of *RAW* was evident right from the start, beginning
with the covers. The size of the magazine made each early cover
a de facto poster. One could easily put on the wall such visually
rich graphics as Joost Swarte's cover for *RAW* no. 2 (an elegant
and intricate fantasy done in the clear line style of Hergé depict-
ing comics-making as a ridiculously complicated industrial
process) or Gary Panter's cover for *RAW* no. 3 (an angry
mohawked punk).

Mouly did the colouring for both covers, in each case finding
a palette to suit the subject: decorous and subtle for Swarte, a
belligerent contrasting of black-and-white with lightning strokes
of other colours for Panter. Panter credited Mouly's colouring
largely for the power of the cover. Chris Ware, arguably the most
renowned artist in the medium today, was profoundly influenced
by the colouring of the Swarte cover. As he told Todd Hignite in
the book *In the Studio*, 'Joost Swarte's amazing cover of *RAW* no.
2 … taught me practically everything I know about colouring
using printing tints, and it was only years later that I found out
that Françoise had coloured the whole thing herself; to this day I
still make use not only of that basic palette, but also the sensibility
of the scheme, with the bright colours being picked out against a
more subdued background.'

Prior to Mouly, almost every other colourist in North American
comics had come out of a garish pulp tradition – a style Mouly
had learned about after a brief spell as a colourist at Marvel in
the late seventies. Spiegelman held the same position before her,
but his attempts at psychedelic pigmentation hadn't gone over
well; at one point, he received a note from Marvel's production
manager telling him that 'Police cars are not pink.' Mouly was
more successful, providing the luminous tints for stories starring

the X-Men, the Fantastic Four and the Black Panther – one comic she coloured featured a battle between the Thing and Brother Voodoo. 'At Marvel, I was getting paid by the page, so I tried to do most books, which were twenty-four to twenty-seven pages, in less than three days,' Mouly recalls. 'I mostly learned by doing. I got to the point where I was dreaming in colours – by which I mean the narrative content of my dreams was interactions between colours.' Colouring had long been a pink-collar ghetto in the comics world, a lowly task cartoonists jobbed off to wives, girlfriends and sisters. Mouly was a pioneer in recognizing that, far from being grunt work, colouring in fact was a significant tool for setting mood.

While Mouly's time at Marvel taught her the traditions of mainstream commercial comics, her sensibility was informed by a host of other diverse (and somewhat more obscure) sources. As with her design sense in general, the Russian constructivists again influenced her ideas of colour and composition. Hampered by Soviet poverty, the constructivists often worked with limited palettes, but the constraint led them to use those colours boldly. In the early issues of *RAW*, Mouly was similarly limited, but took courage and example from what her predecessors had achieved with meagre means. 'The constructivists were what really made me come alive,' she says.

In *RAW*, Mouly and Spiegelman tried to square the circle by issuing a mass-produced magazine that had the quirky individuality of a handmade object. One tactic was tactility: every issue contained an object or physical quirk that required readers to actually touch the magazine. The cover of the first issue included an added-on colour sheet designed to spruce up a black-and-white image (the colour portion of the cover, in keeping with the suicidal theme of the first issue, shows a man jumping from a building). The second issue included a Mark Beyer strip done in the form of bubble-gum cards, which Mouly printed on her press – they inserted a piece of real gum, provided by Spiegelman's long-time employer, Topps, in each stapled bag. For no. 7, part of each cover was torn off and Scotch-taped into a different copy, a wry – and labour-intensive – nod to how magazine distributors tear off the covers of unsold publications.

Mouly, Spiegelman, local contributing artists and a few friends created all this ephemera by hand. Every time an issue was printed, Mouly would carry the boxes up to the fourth-floor walk-up loft, or to the Collective, or sometimes to a corner of the bindery, where they would hold a 'work party' that included the ritual physical modification of the magazine. Making some part of each issue as 'handmade' as possible was part of the magazine's ambition. What held *RAW* together wasn't any particular content repeated issue to issue but rather an underlying sensibility – intense graphics presented in formats that did justice to the uniqueness of the images.

Mouly was famous, perhaps even notorious, for her extreme attention to the printing process. She once told Charles Burns about an argument she had with a printer about the amount of yellow being used on a colour page. While the pressman was out of the room, Mouly climbed up onto the printing press and cranked a wheel for a little bit more yellow. 'You can see her climbing up on this printing press while the guy's in some other room,' Burns says. 'Not taking no for an answer and being fearless about standing up and getting what's going to make the best-looking final piece.' She loved the printers, platemakers and binders she worked with and learned from, and they had an affectionate nickname for her: Frenchy. 'Here's Frenchy that comes to do the stripping' was a common refrain (stripping was the process of laying negatives in place to burn the printing plates). It was, as Mouly recalls, 'a joke they never tired of, even if it wasn't that great to begin with.' Behind the joke was the fact that Mouly was respected by the pressmen as a kindred spirit; they knew her as a skilled businessperson and book maker who took a hands-on approach to every aspect of the process.

Gary Panter describes Mouly and Spiegelman as 'two super-intelligent people forming one mind,' but one can hazard a few rough speculations about the sensibility Mouly brought to *RAW*. From both *Mad* and the undergrounds, Spiegelman had absorbed a certain satirical, belittling aesthetic, one that focused on cutting human aspirations down to size. It's not surprising that his longest sustained narrative involves a tale of rodents, albeit wonderfully humanized ones – his genius is to marry the satirical comics tradition with the inventive formal playfulness of modern art. Mouly's training in the European Beaux-Arts tradition, on the other hand, made her more responsive to physical beauty, to images that have an eye-pleasing surface or panache, a visual flamboyance or joie de vivre. This quality is especially evident in the European cartoonists recruited for *RAW*. Perhaps one of Mouly's most important contributions to *RAW* is white space, of which there had been precious little in underground comics: Mariscal, Meulen and Swarte can make your eyes dance with delight in a way that their North American counterparts rarely do.

Because Spiegelman was busy with both *Maus* and his job at Topps during most of the years *RAW* was being published, Mouly was much more involved in the editing of the magazine, and especially in its physical production. She was also the designer and the publisher who ran the business. This was crucial because the care that *RAW* put into design overturned the world of comics, which had previously been dominated by tawdry ephemerality or ghastly garishness (as in the overripe comics that Hugh Hefner published in *Playboy*, some of them sadly the products of Spiegelman's old mentor Harvey Kurtzman during his long creative twilight).

Mouly's care for design, for matching form to content, can be seen not just in *RAW* but also in the RAW One Shot books that she published and designed, as well as co-edited, notably Gary Panter's *Jimbo*, Sue Coe's *How to Commit Suicide in South Africa* and Jerry Moriarty's *Jack Survives*. Altogether there were ten RAW books, with an average of one being released every year in the 1980s. Unlike *Maus*, these books were not graphic novels per se: rather than trying to mimic the narrative density of a novel in comics form, they tended to focus on the creation of searing and unnerving images.

The Panter book is typical in its oddness. The accident at Three Mile Island had happened in 1979, and anxiety about nuclear apocalypse is a theme of the book, so Mouly and Spiegelman wanted to highlight the resiliency of Panter's images by

First page from Gary Panter's 'Jimbo Erectus' from *RAW* no. 4 (1982). Panter's 'ratty' pen line, splattering of ink all over the page and eschewal of narrative conventions have influenced two generation of cartoonists. Panter's looseness defined the opposite end of the visual spectrum from Burns's tight control.

delivering a 'post-nuclear hardcover.' The cover was made of corrugated cardboard and featured a hand-pasted black, white and red sticker with the title character Jimbo on it. (The format was influenced by several things, including Mouly's own notebooks and an Italian cookbook that Spiegelman found at a bookstore that had a cardboard cover).

In the 1988 documentary *Comic Book Confidential*, Mouly noted that her experiments with different prints and formats often puzzled the craftsmen she worked with. 'When I talked to the binder about [the *Jimbo* book], he couldn't believe it,' she said. 'He couldn't understand the cheapness of the material. "This looks like a throwaway," [he said]. And still we were doing all the printing and everything with this incredible amount of care. For him, it was like an experiment to drive him crazy. He didn't think I had any other purpose in life but to confuse the hell out of him.'

Charles Burns often visited the loft during those years and watched Mouly work: 'Françoise sitting there at a light table with an X-Acto knife, pasting up this thing, trying this thing, doing photocopies, re-editing that, trying a lot of design concepts out, making a dummy of the book or magazine. It was always an ongoing process. I could see the labour involved. This was all pre-digital time. It was very useful for me to witness first-hand a book or a magazine being assembled. Very intense. An incredible amount of work and devotion went into creating this beautiful thing.'

In her design work, Mouly brought to comics an idea that was radically simple: comics are mass-produced visual art, so their printed format is integral to the aesthetic effect they achieve. This core Moulian conviction seems blatantly obvious now: it's the principle that governs the best comics being published in the post-*RAW* generation by firms like Pantheon, Fantagraphics and Drawn and Quarterly. But prior to Mouly, no one had ever applied this concept in a systematic way. In the pre-*RAW* era, design in comics had almost always been an afterthought or an expedient submission to market demands. Through *RAW* and the RAW One Shots, Mouly made care for design and printing priority goals in the comics world.

7

Raw Revolutions

Even as she laboured on the design of the RAW books and magazine, Mouly was helping her artists more and more to shape their narratives. When Charles Burns first started making comics he was, like many cartoonists, more confident in his visual style than in knowing how to tell a story. He had certain thematic interests (imagery taken from horror comics, teenage sexuality and the fear of disease), but his approach to storytelling was largely 'intuitive.' While contributing to *RAW*, he started having conversations with Spiegelman and Mouly that helped the cartoonist think more analytically about narrative.

'There was very specific editing going on, like "This looks really good, but we can't have this," or "This seems clumsy, let's think about other ways this can be approached." Which at that point in my life was very useful and helpful. Their ideas weren't like "This is going to sell more copies because it has more tits and ass or you didn't show anyone smoking dope." It wasn't that. It was "What makes this a better story, why is this more cohesive, why is this more interesting, what can you do to shift this around?" I was certainly at a point in my life when I was trying to learn those things.'

Prior to Mouly, this type of surgical, literary editing of comics simply didn't exist. Spiegelman's earlier editing had been a matter of pushing artists to do better work, but not specifically advising them on the nuts and bolts of narrative. Spiegelman's mentor, Kurtzman, although a titanic editorial influence, was also much more blunt in his approach. Much of Kurtzman's editing consisted of bending a particular artist's skills so he would do what Kurtzman wanted. This led to the creation of superb comics, but they were all Kurtzman-inflected, while the artists Mouly works with retain their individuality and autonomy. (Kurtzman himself, ironically, was ruined by heavy-handed editing from Hugh Hefner, who might be called Kurtzman's Kurtzman). Mouly feels it helps that she doesn't present herself as an artist. Spiegelman's editorial suggestions can be blunt, and *Arcade* had shown that artists often resent being edited by their peers. When communicating with artists, Mouly always goes out of her way to help them preserve a sense of ownership and control.

RAW was a singular mixture of visual diversity and thematic unity. The sheer range of cartooning styles featured in the magazine, often by artists premiering their work, is astonishing. As a showcase, *RAW* presented artists as far apart as Mark Beyer (whose primitive drawings feel like a primal scream), Ever Meulen (a master of panache), Charles Burns (who distills the essence of commercial comics in a perfectly embalmed style), Sue Coe (who redeemed agitprop by giving it a queasy gloss of decaying flesh) and Lynda Barry (whose gnarly drawings and narrative voice perfectly capture what it feels like to be a teenager).

For Chris Ware, who started reading *RAW* in 1983 as a teenager and who would later contribute to it, Mouly and Spiegelman were 'the masters of creating a work of art through editing. The magazine itself was obviously an anthology of individual artists' work but, as a whole, every single issue has an identity, everything fits together as an organism. I can't think of too many people who preceded them who were able to do that, at least in a visual way. There are so many ways comics can abrade each other when placed across the page from one another, from something as simple as clashing colours or styles to whether the stories compliment or contradict each other, either of which can be an asset.'

Since styles were bound to clash, Mouly and Spiegelman sometimes highlighted the radical visual disjunction in their magazine by placing next to each other the pieces that had the sharpest visible contrast. In issue no. 5, the centrefold is a Pascal Doury visual explosion, a scene of carnage that covers nearly the whole page with cross-hatched lines, followed by a sleekly minimalist Joost Swarte page – sequencing designed to produce aesthetic sparks. In assembling the magazine, Mouly and Spiegelman spent endless hours debating the ordering of stories, making dummy after dummy in order to figure out the ideal reading experience.

The ideal reader of *RAW* is one who thinks about not just each individual story but how they all fit together. The easiest connection to make is the recurring themes: suicide, urban despair, the impact of architectural structures on individual psychology, the view of America through foreign eyes, the degrading effects of mass culture, and the mutability and fragility of flesh. It was a magazine made by many hands, but the recurrence of these themes, in a plurality of forms, made evident that it was also thoroughly shaped by the personal concerns of its editors. If the Art Spiegelman of the 1970s was an isolated artist, in *RAW* he found his community.

The magazine also had a distinct political edge. Starting publication in the year Reagan was elected president, it offered mordant commentary on an increasingly conservative America. Throughout its run, *RAW* mocked Cold War paranoia, patriotic triumphalism and media manipulation. Working closely with Sue Coe, Mouly took up the anti-Apartheid cause in South Africa in a decade when the American government remained closely allied with the Boer Republic. Coe's 1983 RAW book, *How to Commit Suicide in South Africa*, wasn't just an art book but advocacy for a particular form of activism: the boycotting of companies that did business with South Africa. A few years later, Spiegelman himself wouldn't allow *Maus* to be published in the country until the African National Congress told him that they thought the book's anti-racist message might have a positive impact on South African readers.

Mouly had less luck with two other political-themed projects by Sue Coe. Mouly takes the blame for the problems with Sue Coe's *X*, a Malcolm X–inspired suite of images on the themes of racism and oppression. The drawings were stunning, but Mouly couldn't achieve the colour effect she wanted, so the images are muddy. To Mouly, the book looks like 'shit.' Mouly and Coe also wanted to publish a book called *Porkopolis*, an exposé of the meat-packing industry that anticipated many of the ideas of Eric Schlosser's *Fast Food Nation* (2001). Unfortunately, the writer who was supposed to do a text to accompany the art didn't work out, so the project was aborted (although Coe did release a pamphlet called *Porkopolis*).

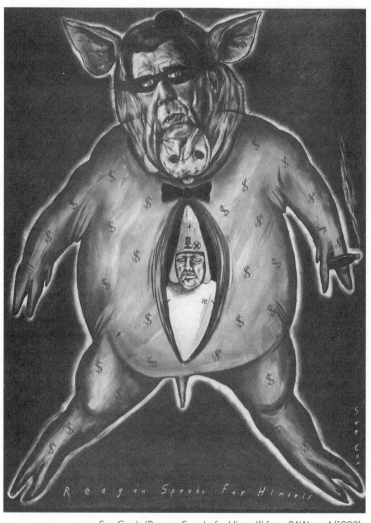

Sue Coe's 'Reagan Speaks for Himself' from *RAW* no. 4 (1982).
Coe's work was the political heart of *RAW.*

'Françoise has the ability not to direct content in a heavy-handed, overbearing way, which would be tedious, boring and eventually unacceptable,' Coe says of the experience. 'There are few art directors or editors who have anything of interest to say about social/political art. It's a play-it-by-numbers kind of career. They don't exist to challenge the system, but to merge with it and cling to corporate jobs. Françoise is subtle in how she manip-ulates – she is conversant with art history.'

Like many artists, Coe loved the attention Mouly gave to the printing process. 'What Françoise did was go to the printers, stay at the printers, and control every aspect of the printing process. She really studied how printing works.'

For the books they worked on together, Coe credits Mouly with figuring out the best way to sequence a suite of images so they would have a maximum effect. 'Françoise has never attempted improvements,' Coe insists. 'What she has done is take all the work in a series and figure out how the puzzle pieces will make a coherent whole. This is something I have trouble doing. I would bring the work over, huge drawings in a roll, throw them on the floor, and she and the cat would circle them like French sharks. Her insight, with my work, is more about ideology than art making. I would look forward to seeing her reactions to the huge drawings on the floor. It was like a magic carpet, would she step on it or not? My best work, which came partially from Françoise's influence, was never published or edited by Françoise at either the *New Yorker* or *RAW*. It was the slaughterhouse work, which later became the book *Dead Meat* and, more recently, the book *Cruel*. Françoise expected me to get into secret places and draw, places where anyone would dread to go to.'

RAW magazine was a critical success and also did surprisingly well commercially. The first issue had a print run of 5,000 copies, which quickly sold out. Within just a few issues, that print run had tripled to 15,000. But it wasn't completely embraced by the comics community. In 1981, Robert Crumb launched a magazine called *Weirdo*, which he described as an attempt to make 'an *Arcade*-type magazine' – a somewhat ironic ambition given his stated reservations about *Arcade* – and which was pointedly designed to be an alternative to *RAW*. In a 1986 interview with the *Comics Journal*, Crumb said, '*RAW* is much more serious, more precious about the work. I never wanted *Weirdo* to be like that; I always wanted it to be a loose and wacky thing ... [*RAW* is] an art object. *Weirdo* is just a sleazy *Mad* imitation.' As its name suggests, *Weirdo* specialized in outsider art, often primitive and crudely transgressive in the mode of the traditional undergrounds (although, intriguingly, this wasn't true of Crumb's own work for the magazine, which tended to be reflective autobiographical pieces, adaptations of literary classics or thoughtful essays).

The militantly lowbrow stance adopted by *Weirdo* didn't just stand in opposition to *RAW* but also demonstrated that the rowdy tradition of underground comics still had its own vitality. 'There was a little regressive aspect to *Weirdo*,' says Bill Griffith. 'It was trying to be a classic underground comic with minimal editorial control.'

This characterization is unfair to *Weirdo*, the best stories of which possessed naked urgency and expressive energy, but it's certainly the case that if *Weirdo* gave evidence of the revitalization of the underground tradition, *RAW* represented an evolution in the creation of comics. The contrast between *Weirdo* and *RAW* that was frequently made in the eighties is, to some degree, an unhelpful comparison, not just because the magazines had different intents but also because there was some overlap in contributors. Not only did Burns, Friedman and Kaz all contribute to *Weirdo*, but Crumb himself did a *RAW* cover and published in Mouly and Spiegelman's magazine a terrific story about the blues musician Jelly Roll Morton.

The pseudo-conflict between *Weirdo* and *RAW* was often exaggerated by artists who felt alienated by what they perceived as Spiegelman and Mouly's highbrow agenda. In a 1989 interview with *Blab* magazine, a digest-size publication devoted to the tradition of transgressive underground comics, Crumb's sentiments were echoed by Daniel Clowes, then a rising star in the alternative comics world. Asked if he liked *RAW*, Clowes responded, 'Not especially ... I mean Spiegelman's a very clever guy. I'm not sure

JELLY ROLL MORTON'S
VOODOO CURSE

BROADWAY   42

WHAT WAS IT THAT SHADOWED "MR. JELLY ROLL", NUMBER ONE HOT BAND LEADER OF THE 'TWENTIES, WHEN HE MOVED TO NEW YORK AT THE PEAK OF HIS POPULARITY AROUND 1928?

IN MAY, 1938, AFTER YEARS OF BEING ON THE SKIDS, MORTON SAT DOWN IN FRONT OF A MICROPHONE AT THE LIBRARY OF CONGRESS AND BEGAN TELLING HIS LIFE STORY TO FOLKSONG COLLECTOR ALAN LOMAX.

BEING FROM NEW ORLEANS, MORTON KNEW ALL ABOUT THE WORKINGS OF VOODOO, AND IN HIS OWN WORDS HE DESCRIBED HOW THESE MYSTERIOUS FORCES WERE USED TO BRING ABOUT HIS DOWNFALL....

©R.CRUMB '84

WAS IT REAL? OR WAS IT... ALL IN HIS MIND?

WHEN I WAS A YOUNG MAN, THESE HOODOO PEOPLE WITH THEIR UNDERGROUND STUFF HELP ME ALONG. I DID NOT FEEL GRATEFUL AND I DID NOT REWARD THEM FOR THE HELP THEY GAVE. NOW, WHEN EVERYTHING BEGAN TO GO AGAINST ME, THOSE UNDERGROUND STREAMS WERE RUNNING AGAINST ME TOO.

I WAS IN THE MUSIC PUBLISHING BUSINESS. EVERYBODY WAS WRITING ME FOR BANDS AND FOR MUSIC AND FOR RADIO PROGRAMS, AND I HAD MORE WORK THAN I COULD DO.

I BUMPED INTO A WEST-INDIAN GUY WHO WAS FOOLING AROUND WITH THE MUSIC PUBLISHING BUSINESS IN AN OFFICE SO SMALL YOU COULDN'T TURN AROUND IN IT.

The first page of Robert Crumb's 'Jelly Roll Morton's Voodoo Curse' from *RAW* no. 7 (1985). Although less famous than his psychedelic work from the 1960s, Crumb's comic strips about blues musicians are among his best work.

if he planned it all out this way or whether he just lucked into it, but he found a good way to package comics – as a magazine the SoHo crowd is proud to have lying at the foot of their loft beds, or whatever. It's an object that people like to own and show off, rather than a sleazy comic to hide behind the radiator.' In the pages of his comic *Eightball*, Clowes parodied Spiegelman as 'Gummo Bubbleman,' a pretentious fraud who locks artists in his loft and makes them produce incomprehensible pseudo-art. (Clowes was far from alone in portraying *RAW* as being a product of Spiegelman alone; throughout the run of *RAW*, Mouly's contribution was generally ignored by critics and outside observers.)

Clowes later revised his opinion of the magazine. 'When the first two or three issues of *RAW* came out in the early eighties, I couldn't have been more excited about it,' Clowes says. 'To all of a sudden be introduced to Friedman, Burns, Kaz, Newgarden, Katchor, Beyer, Moriarty, among many others, was unprecedented. I had never felt any real connection to any school of cartooning before that (I liked the undergrounds, of course, but hated hippies, pot smoking, communes, etc.) but this felt like a new generation – my generation – had arrived en masse with fully formed, highly individual styles. However, after a few issues I started to feel alienated by what seemed like an insular, impenetrable world that would have no place for the kinds of comics I wanted to do: longer stories, humour, etc. My negative reaction was based purely on feelings of pre-emptive rejection – not that I ever actually submitted anything! – and as a way of dealing with the pain of knowing there was this club I wanted so badly to join, but lacked the skills to do so.'

Chris Ware was never among the critics of *RAW*, and is in fact one of the best arguments for the importance of the magazine. As an undergraduate at the University of Texas, Ware produced a comic strip for the student newspaper. A fragment of a Ware strip appeared on the opposite side of the page of an interview with Spiegelman; when Spiegelman saw the clipping of his interview, he was impressed by Ware's art, tracked down the young cartoonist and asked him to contribute to *RAW*. Ware was flabbergasted – he didn't think he would be ready for *RAW* for many years.

Gary Panter has more than once praised Ware as 'a one-man *RAW*.' Many aspects of Ware's aesthetic – his endless formal experimentation, his playing with the shape and size of comics, his concern for production values, even his interest in the nexus between architecture and comics – come from *RAW*. (By some cosmic fluke, the cartoonist's name even contains the mirror image of the magazine: WARe = RAW). Read through the entire run of *RAW* and then Ware's work – it's quickly evident that much of his career has been spent absorbing and synthesizing the lessons of the former.

'*RAW* was unfairly characterized as elitist,' Ware notes. 'It was strange and interesting but certainly human. It's really astonishing when you think of the variety of experimentation and genuine expression that was going on in those periodicals. No one had ever seen fictional comics written with the depth of detail and human complexity of Ben [Katchor], no one had ever seen comics expressionism before Gary Panter, no one had seen work with the ideogrammatic clarity of Charles Burns before. I had no doubt it was the absolute pinnacle of the form, experimentally. I thought about Kaz and Mark Beyer and Charles Burns and Gary [Panter] and Art [Spiegelman] and everyone in the magazine constantly when I was trying to learn how to draw comics; I was consciously trying to understand the lessons of everything they did and some-how put it all together into a single approach of my own.'

Maus was serialized in *RAW* and is undoubtedly the most famous work to come out of the magazine. While we now take the inevitability of *Maus* being published for granted, the book itself could hardly have existed if not for the home provided for it by *RAW* over the thirteen years it took to complete. Earlier, Spiegelman had considered serializing it in the French comics magazine *À Suivre*, but they wanted a story that would run monthly, far too fast for Spiegelman's working methods. *RAW* was published irregularly, averaging an issue a year, a more suitable pace.

When Spiegelman started shopping *Maus* around to publishers in 1983, he was met with widespread bafflement and a stack of rejection letters. The legendary agent Scott Meredith, who

The first page of Chris Ware's 'Thrilling Adventure Stories' from *RAW*, vol. 2, no. 3 (1991). A study in the contrast between form and content: the words are an account of a contemporary boy grappling with his family's racism while the images are a pastiche of a 1930s adventure comics (in the style of Superman co-creator Joe Shuster).

represented writers from Norman Mailer to Philip K. Dick, said, 'If anybody buys that, I'll eat my hat!' Robert Gottlieb of Knopf praised *Maus* as 'clever and funny' but said they were already committed to 'publishing several comic strip-cartoon type books.' Hilary Hinzmann of W. W. Norton said that the narrative was 'more like that of a situation comedy than seems right' for the subject matter.

Eventually, however, Pantheon agreed to publish it, largely because of a glowing 1985 *New York Times* essay that critic Ken Tucker published about Spiegelman's work-in-progress. Spiegelman had been pushing Pantheon to publish the first volume of *Maus* during this time (in part because he was worried that a rumoured Hollywood animated cartoon about Jewish immigrant mice would steal his thunder). Pantheon was initially reluctant and wanted to wait to commit till Spiegelman had finished the entire graphic novel, but the strength of Tucker's enthusiasm – 'a remarkable feat of documentary detail and novelistic vividness,' he raved – and the growing legions of *RAW* fans who had closely followed the serialization won them over.

Much has been written about *Maus*, but a fresh point can be made about how Spiegelman linked form with content, influenced clearly by Mouly's obsessive concern with finding the ideal physical analogue for each comic. A critical part of the narrative hinges on Spiegelman's anger at his father Vladek for destroying his late mother's diary – Spiegelman goes so far as to call his father a murderer. Spiegelman has said that he eschewed a more elaborate visual style for the project because he wanted both the drawings and lettering to have the intimacy of a diary. In size and shape, *Maus* does in fact resemble a diary, especially in the most recent *Complete Maus* hardcover. *Maus* is in effect a replacement for Anja Spiegelman's destroyed diary. The form of the book is intimately tied to the story told in it.

RAW ceased publication in 1991, in large part because Mouly and Spiegelman felt they had succeeded so well in their ambitions that the magazine no longer seemed as urgent. But Mouly also had her mind, and heart, on other things. The couple's daughter,

Nadja, had been born in 1987, and their son, Dashiell, in 1991. Nadja's birth also coincided with a major change in the running of *RAW*. Penguin Books offered to handle the production and distribution of the magazine, which promised a larger audience but also meant that Mouly no longer had the complete hands-on control she once enjoyed. Under the Penguin banner, three trade paperback–size issues of *RAW* came out, closer in appearance to literary journals like the *Paris Review* rather than the earlier tabloid format. Those issues tended to focus more on narrative instead of intense imagery. During this period, the books Mouly and Spiegelman edited were now being co-published by Pantheon working with RAW Books and Graphics. It was a bittersweet triumph: their publishing agenda was being absorbed by the mainstream, but with a loss of the do-it-yourself spirit that animated the early years of Mouly's publishing efforts.

Motherhood, Mouly says, was a 'transformative experience. It answered a lot of existential questions. I was happy to be a woman from the moment I had kids. Before then, being a woman meant limitations in travel and work.' She avoided hiring nannies or au pairs because to her that would have meant 'sharing the love' of her kids. But even as she put in countless hours looking after her kids, she never wanted to give up her artistic pursuits. A young Nadja once observed that one of her friends 'has a mommy all the time.' But for Mouly, giving up all her work for motherhood was never an option; believing that fulfilled adults make the best parents, she continued her intellectual pursuits and even branched out into new areas.

Professionally, Mouly wasn't entirely certain what she wanted to do next. Spurred on by the research she was doing while working with Sue Coe on her political books, Mouly had started taking science classes at Hunter College, with a thought to pursuing studies in neuroscience. While she loved being a student, she abandoned her studies when Dash was born.

Maus, which won a special Pulitzer Prize in 1992, had proven that a serious graphic novel could be a commercial and cultural hit. The last three issues of *RAW* were published by Penguin. Key *RAW* contributors like Panter, Ware, Burns and Katchor were now making up the core of Pantheon's emerging, and very successful, graphic novel line. These *RAW* artists and others were increasingly infiltrating the broader culture, with their work showing up in everything from mainstream magazines to university reading lists and elite galleries. A decade later, the graphic novel section would be a mainstay of almost every bookstore and library.

The eleven issues of *RAW* published between 1980 and 1991 remain an unparalleled, multifaceted achievement. It was a truly international magazine, offering North Americans a window onto the best European work; the late Kim Thompson, who helped translate European comics for *RAW*, continued to translate and publish those same foreign artists at Fantagraphics until his death in the summer of 2013. *RAW* also gave readers, through its translation of the disquieting dreamlike work of Yoshiharu Tsuge, a rare glimpse into the world of sophisticated manga. It would take other publishers decades to start exploring the global riches hinted at in *RAW*.

Spiegelman and Mouly had impeccable taste, and several of the artists who appeared in *RAW* would go on to have major careers – notably Lynda Barry, Gary Panter, Charles Burns, Chris Ware and Ben Katchor. As an assembly of cartooning talent in a single publication, *RAW* has never been equalled. But those artists represent only a small portion of the high-calibre work that filled the pages of *RAW*. As with all important magazines, it was more than the sum of strong individual pieces. *RAW* had a gestalt, a totalizing experience that came not from even its strongest stories but from all this material being gathered together and presented in a magazine where every physical element (the sturdy paper stock, the type, the sequence of stories, the very size of the publication) was born of careful thought and planning.

Mouly's contributions to *RAW* were absolutely essential to its achievement. The magazine was Mouly's idea; she pushed for it over Spiegelman's initial trepidation. It was Mouly's intimate attention to production that made the magazine such a physically beautiful object. It was Mouly's sensitivity to graphic design that gave the magazine a flair that distinguished it from any earlier comics. It was Mouly's French background that brought to the magazine the best European work being done and gave *RAW* its unique international dimension. And, finally, Mouly's architectural training contributed an integral strand to the magazine's aesthetic DNA, fostering an obsessive concern with urban landscapes and the repeated investigation into the formalist connections between comics and architecture – a linkage that became a major thematic concern in such *RAW* artists as Katchor and Ware.

From the start, Mouly had a premonition that *RAW* would have a seismic effect on the larger culture. In a 1980 interview with the *Comics Journal*, conducted right before the publication of the second issue of *RAW*, Mouly made a strikingly prescient prediction: 'We expect two things to happen in the future as offspring of *RAW*. Magazines that already print comics will, I think, widen the range of comics that they print as a result of *RAW*. Magazines that do not print comics may start printing comics, because they might see different possibilities that relate more to their editorial approach.'

Mouly had a good crystal ball. Over the next two decades, several *RAW* cartoonists (and other cartoonists shaped by the *RAW* aesthetic) found work in such unlikely venues as *Time* magazine, the *New York Times Magazine*, *Details*, the *Virginia Quarterly Review* and *Harper's*. But in 1980, did even Mouly guess that the one magazine that would so enthusiastically adopt the *RAW* aesthetic would be the *New Yorker*? And that she would play such a decisive role in that transformation?

Joost Swarte's cover for *RAW* no. 2 (1980), drawn with a clean architectural precision that recalls Hergé's *Tintin*, imagines what it would be like if a comic strip were produced by the same industrial process that goes into filmmaking. The central image was coloured by Françoise Mouly, while Swarte made the strap on the left, itself a tour de force of hand-cut Zip-A-Ton pieces.

Gary Panter's cover for *RAW* no. 3 (1981) was originally a black-and-white drawing, repurposed by Françoise Mouly and Art Spiegelman. Colour by Mouly.

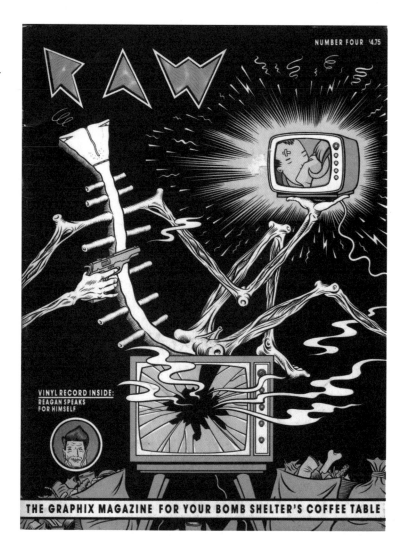

Charles Burns's die-cut cover for *RAW* no. 4 (1982). Both the image of Reagan and the couple on the television screen are actually from the second full-colour cover beneath this one. Both the anatomical focus and the critique of Reagan are strong thematic concerns in *RAW*.

Ever Meulen's cover for *RAW* no. 5 (1983) plays with intersecting picture planes in the manner of M. C. Escher, but with a jaunty cartooning style. The cover contains many pictures within pictures.

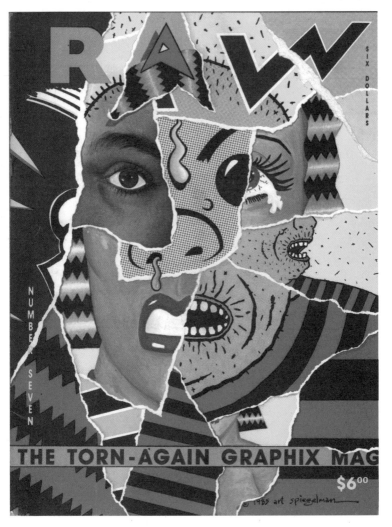

Art Spiegelman's cover for *RAW* no. 7 (1985). The theme of the cover and the issue is tearing. The right eye is from a photograph of Mouly. The upper-right corner of each cover was torn and taped inside a different copy from the same print run.

Table of contents for *RAW* no. 7, designed by Françoise Mouly, with a space for the torn-off corner of another copy of the magazine to be taped in.

New Yorker cover dated September 24, 2001, titled *9/11/2001*. Created in collaboration by Art Spiegelman and Françoise Mouly. One of the most famous *New Yorker* covers grew out of the conflict between the demand for an image to comment on the events of 9/11 and the feeling that no image could do it justice.

Françoise Mouly's cover for the October 18, 2004, issue, titled
A Shadow over the Election. On the eve of the re-election of George W. Bush,
Mouly offered a sober commentary on the tortures of Abu Ghraib
casting a shadow on America's reputation.

PRICE $3.99   THE   MAY 29, 2006

NEW YORKER

Called *Losing Face*, this is Mouly's cover from May 29, 2006.
A Memorial Day cover, with the missing face of Uncle Sam
suggesting the lack of any patriotic rationale for contemporary wars.

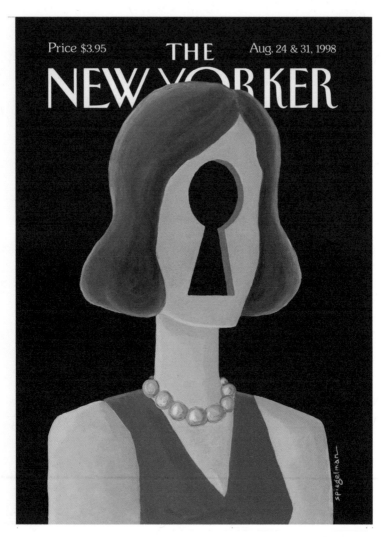

Spiegelman's cover for August 24 & 31, 1998, titled *Private Lives*.
Another example of the evocatory power of a missing face.
Other magazines have photos of celebrity faces,
the *New Yorker* makes readers fill in the blanks.

Saul Steinberg cover, dated April 25, 1994, titled *Main Street*.
What the modernists did to writing, Steinberg did to magazine covers:
he created a poetics of luminous details and radical disjunction.
Steinberg's aesthetic has profoundly influenced Mouly and
countless *New Yorker* artists.

Sept. 15, 1997 THE Price $2.95
NEW YORKER

R. Sikoryak's cover dated September 15, 1997, titled *Last Salute*.
To mark the death of Princess Diana, Mouly preferred a crayon-y image,
pregnant with meaning, rather than a polished illustration.

Barry Blitt's cover for July 21, 2008, titled *The Politics of Fear*.
A satire on right-wing paranoia about then-presidential candidate
Barack Obama's alleged foreignness and radicalism. Perhaps the most
controversial *New Yorker* cover ever, in part because, Mouly argues,
it brought inchoate fears out into the open where they could be mocked.

reason to be proud of her career. 'I have a sense of having really achieved what I set out to do thirty-five or more years ago, even if it has been invisible to the world at large,' Mouly writes. 'I wanted to find something big, a goal that was mine, something that no one else would do. And it was okay with me if the only ego gratification was accomplishment. That, of course, led to *RAW* and the RAW One-Shots. It was complicated, but it gave me a way to articulate my vision.'

When asked to talk about her sense of accomplishment, Mouly turns once again to the central idea that her love of art stems from her love of Art: 'Art is the one who articulated it best. A few years ago, just as he was going into the dentist's chair, teenage Nadja asked him: "Papa, what is art?" And, being who he is, he came out with the answer: "Art is giving shape to one's thoughts and feelings."' For Mouly, that may have been the most revolutionary, mind-opening notion she espoused when she met and fell in love with Art. That art isn't just what other people call art, what gets validated by critics' opinions, but that comics can be a means of self-expression, and so can editing.

'In the past two or three years, I have started using the first person, calling myself an artist, taking credit for my work (such as the *Blown Covers* book),' she continues. 'The courage for it came from, first, the success of *RAW*, then the new-found confidence and peace I made with myself when I became a mother, and a sense of accomplishment at the *New Yorker* – I do believe I'm harnessing the power of artists as catalysts, holding a mirror to society, producing a suite of images, that, taken as a whole, capture what we're going through. Then the setting up of RAW Junior in 1998, where I bucked a lot of prejudices head on: "If it's educational, it can't be art or literature," and "If it's for children, it can't be art because you're catering to a specific audience," but now we're bringing comics into the classroom, which was inconceivable then, so I know I succeeded in making a change for the better. And, finally, the 9/11 cover. In the three or four days after the tragedy, I pursued my guts' feelings in spite of everyone else's agenda. It was a terrifying moment, maybe as terrifying as the time at the YMCA when I first arrived in New York. I was utterly lost, yet I had the responsibility of coming up with a statement. I had to buck everyone else's idea of what I should do – editors who wanted a photo and Art who wanted his own image published. But I'm glad I made that leap of faith in myself.'

Françoise Mouly was twenty-two when she launched RAW Books and Graphics. She is now fifty-seven years old and very much in mid-career. In the corridors of the *New Yorker*, she sometimes sees colleagues three or more decades older than she is who still contribute to the magazine. She's overturned the world of comics and graphic design more than once, and one wonders what challenge she'll take on next. The only sure thing is that like all the other projects that she's worked on, her future work will bear the stamp of an editorial vision that has few equals.

Works Consulted

Adler, Renata. *Gone: The Last Days of 'The New Yorker.'* New York: Simon and Schuster, 1999.

Burns, Charles. Interview by the author, May 20, 2013.

Brunetti, Ivan. Email to the author, June 5, 2013.

Cavalieri, Joey. 'Jewish Mice, Bubblegum Cards, Comics Art, and Raw Possibilities: An Interview with Art Spiegelman and Françoise Mouly,' in *The Comics Journal* no. 65, August 1981.

Clowes, Daniel. Interview by the author, May 27, 2013.

Coe, Sue. Interview with the author, July 22, 2013.

Gill, Brendan. *Here at 'The New Yorker'.* New York: Random House, 1975.

Griffith, Bill. Interview by the author, April 25, 2013.

Groth, Gary et al. 'Slaughter on Greene Street: Art Spiegelman and Françoise Mouly Talk about *RAW*,' in *The Comics Journal* no. 74, August 1982.

Groth, Gary. 'Politics, Pinheads and Post-Modernism: Bill Griffith Interview,' in *The Comics Journal* 157, March 1993.

Kartalopoulos, Bill. 'A *RAW* History,' in *Indy* magazine, Winter 2005. (Note: this ran online but is no longer available in its original web form. It will be incorporated into a forthcoming book).

Kinsley, Michael. 'Department of Amplification,' in *The New Republic*, July 16, 1984.

Kunz, Anita. Email to the author, July 21, 2013.

Macrone, Michael. 'Two Generations of *Weirdo*: An Interview With R. Crumb and Peter Bagge,' in *The Comics Journal* no. 106, March 1986.

Menand, Louis. 'A Friend Writes,' in *The New Republic*, Feb 26, 1990.

Mouly, Françoise. *Blown Covers: 'New Yorker' Covers You Were Never Meant to See.* New York: Abrams, 2012.

———. Numerous interviews and emails with author, January–July 2013.

Mouly, Francoise and Art Spiegelman. *Little Lit: Folklore and Fairy Tale Funnies.* New York: HarperCollins, 2000.

———. *Little Lit: Strange Stories for Strange Kids.* New York: HarperCollins, 2001.

—————. *Little Lit: It Was a Dark and Silly Night...* New York: Harper-Collins, 2003.

Mouly, Françoise and Lawrence Weschler. *Covering 'The New Yorker': Cutting Edge Covers from a Literary Institution.* New York: Abbeville Press, 2000.

Panter, Gary. Email to the author, June 12, 2013.

Rosenkranz, Patrick. *Rebel Visions: The Underground Comix Revolution, 1963–1975.* Seattle: Fantagraphics, 2008.

Scholz, Carter. 'Raw Roots,' in *The Comics Journal* no. 64, July 1981.

Sikoryak, Robert. Interview with the author. May 1, 2013.

Spiegelman, Art. *Breakdowns: Portrait of the Artist as a Young %@&*!.* New York: Pantheon Books, 2008.

—————. *Breakdowns: From Maus to Now.* New York: Belier Press, 1977.

—————. *MetaMaus.* New York: Pantheon Books, 2011.

—————. Numerous interviews and emails with author, January–July 2013.

Tucker, Ken. 'Cats, Mice and History,' in *New York Times Book Review*, May 26, 1985.

Updike, John. Foreword to *The Complete Book of Covers from 'The New Yorker,' 1925–1989.* New York: Alfred A. Knopf, 1989.

Viva, Frank. Interview with the author. May 11, 2013.

Ware, Chris. Interview with author. May 20, 2013.

Witek, Joseph (ed.). *Art Spiegelman: Conversations.* Jackson: University Press of Mississippi, 2007.

Books and magazines edited by Françoise Mouly and Art Spiegelman as an outgrowth of *RAW*:

RAW Volume 1, eight issues published by RAW Books and Graphics, 1980–1986.

RAW Volume 2, three issues published by Penguin Books, 1989–1991.

The majority of the first three issues of *RAW* Volume 1 was reprinted in a book edited by Mouly and Spiegelman titled *Read Yourself Raw* (New York: Pantheon, 1987).

The following books, listed in chronological order, were edited by Mouly and Spiegelman, with the exception of the Ben Katchor book, which was edited by Spiegelman and R. Sikoryak:

Panter, Gary. *Jimbo*. New York: RAW Books and Graphics, 1982.

Coe, Sue (with Holly Metz). *How to Commit Suicide in South Africa*. New York: RAW Books and Graphics, 1983.

Moriarty, Jerry. *Jack Survives*. New York: RAW Books and Graphics, 1984.

Panter, Gary. *Invasion of the Elvis Zombies*. New York: RAW Books and Graphics, 1984.

Burns, Charles. *Big Baby*. New York: RAW Books and Graphics, 1986.

Coe, Sue (with Art Spiegelman and Judith Moore). *X*. New York: RAW Books and Graphics, 1986.

Beyer, Mark. *Agony*. New York: RAW/Pantheon, 1987

Panter, Gary. *Jimbo: Adventures in Paradise*. New York: RAW/Pantheon, 1988

Burns, Charles. *Hard-Boiled Defective Stories*. New York: RAW/Pantheon, 1988.

Katchor, Ben. *Cheap Novelties: The Pleasures of Urban Decay*. New York: Penguin Books, 1991.

TOON Books in order of publication:

Hayes, Geoffrey. *Benny and Penny in Just Pretend*. 2008.

Lynch, Jay and Frank Cammuso. *Otto's Orange Day*. 2008.

Rosenstiehl, Agnès. *Silly Lilly and the Four Seasons*. 2008.

Spiegelman, Art. *Jack and the Box*. 2008.

Davis, Eleanor. *Stinky*. 2008.

Lynch, Jay and Dean Haspiel. *Mo and Jo Fighting Together Forever*. 2008.

Hayes, Geoffrey, *Benny and Penny in The Big No-No!* 2009.

Bliss, Harry. *Luke on the Loose*. 2009.

Smith, Jeff. *Little Mouse Gets Ready*. 2009.

Spiegelman, Nadja and Trade Loeffler. *Zig and Wikki in Something Ate My Homework*. 2010.

Hayes, Geoffrey. *Benny and Penny in the Toy Breaker*. 2010.

Rosenstiehl, Agnès. *Silly Lilly in What Will I Be Today?* 2011.

Coudray, Philippe. *Benjamin Bear in Fuzzy Thinking*. 2011.

Knight, Hilary. *Nina in That Makes Me Mad*. 2011.

Hayes, Geoffrey. *Patrick in a Teddy Bear's Picnic*. 2011.

Johnson, R. Kikuo. *The Shark King*. 2012.

Spiegelman, Nadja and Trade Loeffler. *Zig and Wikki in The Cow*. 2012.

Ponti, Claude. *Chick and Chickie Play All Day*. 2012.

Hayes, Geoffrey. *Benny and Penny in Lights Out*. 2012.

Modan, Rutu. *Maya Makes a Mess*. 2012.

Viva, Frank. *A Trip to the Bottom of the World with Mouse*. 2012.

Nytra, David. *The Secret of the Stone Frog*. 2012.

French, Renée. *Barry's Best Buddy*. 2013.

Coudray, Philiipppe. *Benjamin Bear in Bright Ideas*. 2013.

Hayes, Geoffrey. *Patrick Eats His Peas and Other Stories*. 2013.

Commuso, Frank and Jay Lynch. *Otto's Backwards Day*. 2013.

Liniers. *The Big Wet Balloon*. 2013.

Credits

P. 10: 'Valentine's Day,' by Art Spiegelman ©1993, Art Spiegelman & *The New Yorker*

P. 87: '9/11/2001,' by Françoise Mouly and Art Spiegelman ©2001, Françoise Mouly, Art Spiegelman & *The New Yorker*

P. 88: 'A Shadow over the Election,' by Françoise Mouly ©2004, Françoise Mouly & *The New Yorker*

P. 89: 'Losing Face,' by Françoise Mouly ©2006, Françoise Mouly & *The New Yorker*

P.90: 'Private Lives,' by Art Spiegelman ©1998, Art Spiegelman & *The New Yorker*

P. 91: 'Main Street,' by Saul Steinberg ©1994, The Saul Steinberg Foundation & *The New Yorker*

P. 92: 'Last Salute,' by R. Sikoryak ©1997, R. Sikoryak & *The New Yorker*

P. 93: 'The Politics of Fear,' by Barry Blitt ©2008, Barry Blitt & *The New Yorker*

P. 94: 'New Yorkistan,' by Maira Kalman & Rick Meyerowitz ©2001, Maira Kalman, Rick Meyerowitz & *The New Yorker*

P. 95 top left: 'Natural Selection,' by Chris Ware ©2010, Chris Ware & *The New Yorker*

P. 95 top right: 'Adaptation,' by Adrian Tomine ©2010, Adrian Tomine & *The New Yorker*

P. 95 bottom left: 'Survival of the Fittest,' by Daniel Clowes ©2010, Daniel Clowes & *The New Yorker*

P. 95 bottom right: 'Biodiversity,' by Ivan Brunetti ©2010, Ivan Brunetti & *The New Yorker*

P. 105: 'The Breakfast Plate,' by David Hockney ©2010, David Hockney & *The New Yorker*

P. 110: 'Wilshire & Lex,' by Saul Steinberg ©1995, The Saul Steinberg Foundation & *The New Yorker*

From other sources

P. 30: Art Spiegelman's 'Prisoner on Planet Hell,' from *Short Order Comix* no. 1 (Head Press, 1973), reprinted in Spiegelman's *Breakdowns* (1977; 2008), ©1973, Art Spiegelman, used by permission

P. 46: from Art Spiegelman's 'Nervous Rex: The Malpractice Suite,' *Arcade* no. 6 (The Print Mint, 1976), reprinted in Spiegelman's *Breakdowns* ©1976, Art Spiegelman, used by permission

P. 50: Flyer for Joost Swart's postcards, produced by RAW Books and Graphics

P. 96: Covers of Renée French's *Barry's Best Buddy* and Frank Viva's *A Trip to the Bottom of the World with Mouse* courtesy of TOON Books

Acknowledgements

While researching this book, I realized that the first time I saw Françoise Mouly's work was in 1978 when I read the Marvel Comics adaptation of Charles Dickens's *A Christmas Carol*, which she coloured. I was eleven years old. Three years later, thanks to a review in the *Comics Journal*, I was introduced to Art Spiegelman's cartooning, including the early chapter of *Maus*, as well as the larger world of *RAW*. So I've been living with the comics Françoise and Art have been bringing into the world for almost my entire conscious life. This book is an attempt to get a measure of their impact on me and the world at large. I couldn't have written it without Françoise and Art being willing to talk to me so extensively and with such candour and intelligence.

Mina Kaneko, Françoise's assistant at the *New Yorker*, has been super helpful in setting up interviews, providing scans and in general making a hectic process run very smoothly. Alexa Rossell and Julia Phillips have been equally crucial with TOON Books assistance.

Thanks to the many artists who I've talked to about Françoise Mouly (not all of whom are quoted in the book): Charles Burns, Ivan Brunetti, Frank Cammuso, Daniel Clowes, Bill Griffith, Anita Kunz, Rutu Modan, Gary Panter, Robert Sikoryak, Sue Coe, Frank Viva and Chris Ware. Many of these artists also graciously granted permission for their art to be reproduced.

A book about publishing and editing can find no better home than Coach House Books, which owns two Heidelberg presses and a superb editorial team. I'm grateful for the prose-trimming and bookmaking acumen of the whole Coach House crew. The manuscript has been improved in innumerable ways by Jason McBride (who helped conceptualize this book), Stuart Ross, Alana Wilcox and Heidi Waechtler. Evan Munday and Leigh Nash's enthusiasm for the project and cleverness about getting the word out about it has been heartening. My only regret with Coach House is that my perpetual tardiness has caused them more stress than any honest publisher deserves. My email folder is littered with apologies I've sent to Coach House, so I'm pleased for once to be able to say thank you rather than sorry.

The Beguiling is more than a comic-book store. For anyone working on a book like this, it is an invaluable archive and source of comics scuttlebutt. A tip of the hat to the staff and to store owner Peter Birkemoe, who lent me some rare issues of *RAW*. By organizing the Toronto Comics Art Festival, Christopher Butcher and Miles Baker allowed me to spend an exhausting and rewarding weekend talking to Mouly and a contingent of her artists.

Thanks to Gary Groth and Eric Reynolds for assistance in getting permission to use Robert Crumb art. Beyond that, I'm grateful to both for the many fine comics they've published over the years.

Let me here light a candle to the memory of their colleague Kim Thompson, who, while I was working on this book, was diagnosed with cancer and died at the tragically young age of fifty-six. Kim not only translated some of the comics that appeared in *RAW*, he was also an immensely important figure in helping make comics truly cosmopolitan. There will be books written about Thompson's legacy.

My thinking about *RAW* has been informed by the massive and splendidly organized oral history of the magazine that Bill Kartalopoulos assembled, which ran in *Indy* magazine in 2005. This oral history is currently in internet limbo but will one day form the core of a book. Out of respect for Bill's work, I've refrained from quoting from the interviews he's conducted and given my own perspective on matters. But the quality of Bill's work needs to be acknowledged.

The interviews Hillary Chute conducted for the book *MetaMaus* were of such consistently high quality I was often tempted to quote them wholesale. I've resisted the urge but remain in her debt. I criticize the *Comics Journal* in the foreword, but it's undeniable that the magazine's three decades of criticism and reporting on comics constitutes the best single historical source we have on the medium.

My understanding of comics is inseparable from my many friendships with people who also love the form. Let me mention Ho Che Anderson, Sarah Brouillette, Chester Brown, Peggy Burns, Jerry Ciccoritti, Tom Devlin, Charles Hatfield, Tim Hodler, Brad Mackay, Dan Nadel, Chris Oliveros, Sean Rogers, Seth, Diana Tamblyn and Kent Worcester. Jessica Johnson, my best friend, deserves a special shout-out for our many conversations about editing, comics, design and the *New Yorker*. For more than a decade, Jessica has lugged her *New Yorker* collection from residence to residence, in no small part because whenever she looks at a cover it conjures up the whole content of the magazine. Her attachment to the *New Yorker* and its covers fortified my convictions about Mouly's accomplishment. Art Goldhammer advised me on French history. Medrie Purdham had some wise thoughts on editing.

In reflecting on editing as I've done while working on this book, I can't help but think that whatever skill I may have as a writer comes from the education I've received from some nurturing and demanding editors, including Andy Lamey, Ian Garrick Mason (whose magazine *Gravitas* published my earliest thoughts on *RAW*), Alex Star (formerly of *Lingua Franca* and the *Boston Globe*), Jennifer Schuessler (also formerly of the *Boston Globe*) and Jared Bland (of the *Globe and Mail*).

This book was written on the move, in Regina and three very different Toronto neighbourhoods (Rexdale, Cabbagetown and the Annex). These moves were made easier thanks to the hospitality of the Ganevs and the Heers. My mother Simer Heer provided much needed babysitting assistance, as did my brother Bob. Aside from being an excellent Chacha to his niece, Bob also gave me with computer assistance and was a great source of comics lore.

My daughter Bella Heer (age two) and niece Avery Soltys (age five) are both fans of the TOON Books line. Their enthusiasm informs the final chapter.

Robin Ganev's role in instigating this book has been alluded to in the introduction. But above and beyond that, there is nothing I'm more grateful for than the life we've built together, which we now share with Bella.

Writing a book based in large part on interviews, I've had to adjudicate between conflicting memories. I've tried to make reasonable judgements, but there are other versions of some of the stories told in this book.

All mistakes in the book are my own.

About the Author

Jeet Heer is a cultural journalist and academic who divides his time between Toronto and Regina. He has written for many publications including the *Globe and Mail*, Slate.com, the *Boston Globe*, the *Walrus*, the *American Prospect*, the *Comics Journal*, the *Virginia Quarterly Review* and the *Guardian of London*. He has co-edited eight books and been a contributing editor to another eight volumes. With Kent Worcester, Jeet co-edited *A Comics Studies Reader* (University Press of Mississippi), which won the Peter C. Rollins Book Award given annually to the best book in American Studies or Cultural Studies. He's been awarded a Fulbright Scholarship. His articles have been anthologized in both *The Best American Comics Criticism* (Fantagraphics) and *The Best Canadian Essays* collection for 2012. With Chris Ware, Jeet continues to edit the *Walt and Skeezix* series from Drawn and Quarterly, which is now entering its sixth volume.

About the
Exploded Views Series

Exploded Views is a series of probing, provocative essays that offer surprising perspectives on the most intriguing cultural issues and figures of our day. Longer than a typical magazine article but shorter than a full-length book, these are punchy salvos written by some of North America's most lyrical journalists and critics. Spanning a variety of forms and genres – history, biography, polemic, commentary – and published simultaneously in all digital formats and handsome, collectible print editions, this is literary reportage that at once investigates, illuminates and intervenes.

Typeset in Goodchild Pro and Gibson Pro. Goodchild was designed by Nick Shinn in 2002 at his ShinnType foundry in Orangeville, Ontario. Shinn's design takes its inspiration from French printer Nicholas Jensen who, at the height of the Renaissance in Venice, used the basic Carloginian minuscule calligraphic hand and classic roman inscriptional capitals to arrive at a typeface that produced a clear and even texture that most literate Europeans could read. Shinn's design captures the calligraphic feel of Jensen's early types in a more refined digital format. Gibson was designed by Rod McDonald in honour of John Gibson FGDC (1928–2011), Rod's long-time friend and one of the founders of the Society of Graphic Designers of Canada. It was McDonald's intention to design a solid, contemporary and affordable sans serif face.

Printed at the old Coach House on bpNichol Lane in Toronto, Ontario, on Rolland Opaque Natural paper, which was manufactured, acid-free, in Saint-Jérôme, Quebec, from 50 percent recycled paper, and it was printed with vegetable-based ink on a 1965 Heidelberg KORD offset litho press. Its pages were folded on a Baumfolder, gathered by hand, bound on a Sulby Auto-Minabinda and trimmed on a Polar single-knife cutter.

Edited by Jason McBride
Designed by Alana Wilcox
Series cover design by Ingrid Paulson, with input from Françoise Mouly
Cover image, 'Industry News and Review No. 6,' by Françoise Mouly, first
    published in *RAW* no. 1 (1980), courtesy of the artist

Coach House Books
80 bpNichol Lane
Toronto ON M5S 3J4
Canada

416 979 2217
800 367 6360

mail@chbooks.com
www.chbooks.com